Many Homes

Jane Hearn

A Harcourt Achieve Imprint

www.Rigby.com
1-800-531-5015

This home was made with brick.

This home was made with wood.

This home was made with metal.

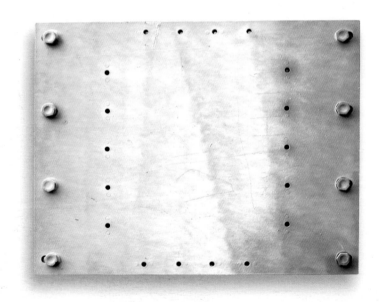

This home was made with stone.

This home was made with straw.

This home was made with grass.

This home was made with ice.

What is this home
made with?